æpoetics

thaddeus conti

ISBN: 1-935084-01-1
ISBN13: 978-1-935084-01-3

back cover photo of thaddeus conti
by craig morse
www.flickr.com/people/culturesubculture

book design
by bill lavender

Lavender Ink

New Orleans

ᘯ

To Anne,

" you've done good raising Peter. "

æpoetics
thaddeus conti

—Thaddeus Conti

13	introduction by david rowe
15	haus
16	blenter
17	*please don't take away my pens*
18	skills
19	sunlights broken column
20	climate before the advent of the plain whiter line
21	*abraxas continued*
22	shrapnel
23	bowing exit stage right
24	bathesheba
25	*wording this wad*
26	somephin mista
27	angel of bad reception
28	hanged
29	*kant o' knees*
30	whimsitudina
31	year of the rooster
32	bathsheba 2
33	dying breed
34	requiem for kindergarten
35	*ramshooken*
36	modern love
37	alchemystic
38	mattress teeth
39	*desdellama*
40	gulp
41	anthropolymorphic madonna
42	when the hammer come down
43	*giving the gave to get what you got*
44	roger and hammerstein's mission to mars
45	mary go down
46	caduseus

47	*generic poetry*
48	**hard road to hoe**
49	**shhh**
50	**strange relation between birds and arrows**
51	**st. of st.**
52	*genufake*
53	**eaglerific**
54	**waaaaaaaa**
55	**point of nomenclature**
56	**gravid heap of televisions**
57	**lost goat**
58	**the awkward position of questioning a shadow**
59	*the many ways to read a word*
60	**a scratch on the record**
61	**literary**
62	**garveled jism and the kiss of a dead man**
63	**ascencion street**
64	*on prayers being answered*
65	**g**
66	**offstandish**
67	**cargo ill**
68	**empish**
69	**germinization**
70	**sir**
71	*pop u lurch*
72	**device conceived to separate space from time**
73	**hoe the holy**
74	**furnit**
75	*consume the moon*
76	**eyes as stars**
77	**fleur**
78	**swiss-saur**
79	**boogalook**
80	*bad news sunshine*

81   jade
82   ode to wdk
83   gazellesque
84   creased
85   untrue melody
86   the reason dentist do themselves in
87   charles fort
88   to the left
89   paddy
90   shut up and write a book
91   for the cop with a rope chain
92   gertrude
93   awakening the sulfur demon
94   played well vs well played
95   warrant applied for
96   the mystic trick of don't try this at home
97   cheeks set to swivel
98   oppositionship
99   vladimir mother vladimirror
100   pass the bottle aristophanes
101   style right
102   the yawning bow of lorca
103   the myth of thin ankles
104   unapproachable
105   subtitularity
106   tecumsah was angered
107   winding a wind
108   whiskied fly
109   pillow crasher
110   dynamite string
111   scuttling space
112   on the occasion of something resembling a title
113   it's his party
114   baba istic

115   blank
116   crude
117   I
118   dino
119   history of the peloponnesian war
120   modern love 2
121   the phenomenon of married couples sharing a resemblance
122   sterile
123   schematic for the physical acoustics of a broken piano string
124   juglefuke
125   the radius of a wish
126   profiles of zero
127   tiny monsters
129   din-din
130   monica
131   patriotic embolism
132   bowied
133   lightening of heaven's lust
134   swack
135   intrusion
136   we are the aliens
137   dogwood
138   also dimensional
139   wompum bucked
140   railing them in
141   redux
142   dog
143   whistfully full of it
144   the nazarene
145   gnash
146   addendum to get an atheist into heaven
147   stoop
148   her knee ate her feet
149   the difference between foreign films and domestic drug use

150 sutured the sill
151 irun
152 bending a mattress
153 abi sade
154 stations of the cross
155 *fragging colonel muster*
156 protocality
157 wextet
158 actio
159 gasha khant
160 *a preemptive meeting of alchoholics anonymous at the satellite gravesite of lord byron*
    without the permission of his estate or the knowledge of the general service committee
161 birthabang
162 keaton
163 quait
164 let the mother fuck circle shit dungaree blu
165 *all I ever needed to know I learned in those first few hours at rehab*
166 blink pitched sideways
167 dismas
168 ted just admit it
169 uniting the dream
170 *impetus*
171 light style
172 speriment
173 the zero hour
174 for L
175 *treason in vaudeville*
176 awkward ascent
177 de mal
178 french waiter
179 totemic
180 *the heart is not a pimple*
181 graduate
182 ro

183	archibal the lessor
184	dragonpubis
185	*plastic is the cotton of the twenty first century*
186	bitch can't hit
187	unsewing a football
188	loaves and fishes
189	the new marble
190	*shamanabalistic*
191	superfluous puncuation
192	she walks these hills
193	permanet press
194	ghosts of the hallway
195	*the demystification of an american teenager turned man*
196	david rowe
197	charlemange
198	wendy and the fly
199	sour stitch
200	*a euclidian recipe of artificial sunlight for the splintered contingency of penthouse forum subscribers*
201	risking a hand
202	napolic
203	carnival grease
204	bombadeer tracts
205	misuse of ink
206	*the sexual prowess of a meteorologist as held over from the age of aquarius*
207	milo
208	early attempt at an artist statement
209	salamandoor
210	nightstood
211	*in times as these*
212	birdlike
213	jumbleish ish
214	madty the madman
215	something the kids will like

216 *apprenticeship as a reason to ride*
219 **salutorious**
220 **staring down hope**
221 **paticiples**
222 **steadmonster**
223 *crack*
225 **fortnightraven**
226 **rock candy**
227 **chalkboard**
228 **contemplative hitler**
229 **sentinel of one**
230 **cuth of moustatrd**
231 **anonomae**
232 **train wreck**
233 **taurus**
234 *highly unscientific search for signs of the oversoul*
235 **nurse the wished upon**
236 **deposition of ink**
237 **five blosoms**
238 **corinthcopia**
239 *treatise*
241 **sad mule**
242 **aglee savage**
243 *knowing the subtle congruency between need and want*
244 **shylock**
245 **bauhaus 97**
246 *lighting a match behind binoculars in an elevator shaft*
247 **pray up in the wind**
248 **rolling space bent**
249 **undersunk**
250 **soped**
251 *talent is not a precursor to sanity*
252 **boogie chile**
253 **wespterly**

254 **coribanticant**
255 **talons**
256 *astroglide for astral plane*
257 **sad time gone**
258 **mussolini breath**
259 **bambent**
260 **waterfall**
261 *the general implication of being*
262 **lanscoped jesus**
263 *the bishop of cantilever and the malaria symphonies*
264 **mentaur**
265 *seemingly impossible retaliation on the incredible hulk by beethoven and the sonatas that followed*
266 **leather**
267 **jesus was no square**
268 *out with an elephant eye*
270 **eyes without ears**
271 *disclosing visions to semi-permanent strangers*
272 **comrade**
273 *the inverse ratio of fellatio to migrant prostitutes*
274 **populorch**
275 **beefed heart**
276 *INVITE TO THE PESTILENT*
280 **broken daisy**
281 **jump jip jump**
282 *libranoia*
285 **taurpion**
286 **poiniot**
287 **formagine**
288 **itsabella**
289 **scarbled**

‡

Introduction

Like Dionysus himself, Thaddeus is twice-born. Seems the first time, in the a.m., he managed to bring the womb along with him. So they stuffed him back in, separated him from the uterine lining, &, in the p.m., re-delivered him. All on a Halloween day in New Orleans. In the devoutly Catholic Conti clan, it's a tradition for the monsignor to name the children. Since the good padre couldn't very well name our protagonist after the dithyrambic god of tantric intoxication, he went with (Jude) Thaddeus, the flame-headed patron of desperate cases & lost causes. In lieu of/en route to being *thrice*-born, he aspires to leave behind- in tubs of Tupperware- ten thousand x-fine pen-&-ink line drawings. "Ten thousand," a literal myriad, since it's Taoist shorthand for all of creation. Unlike the venerable Lao Tzu's however, Thaddeus' pilgrimage is chock-a-block with booby-trap birthday cakes & tenderly-rendered toilet seats, traversed by scorp-ooster-mander kings & prima ballerinas on crack-smoking sabbatical. In Thaddeus' hands, the dignity of the fleur-de-lis is restored: no longer the municipal cliché dangling from every tourist's charm bracelet, it's become once again a thing of power & danger: the brand on the brow of a brigand; Juno's lilystalk used to parthenogenetically pleasure herself; an adamantine trident to rend the veil of illusion or, indeed, to bring about St. Jude Thaddeus' martyrdom. Having shared with him a suburban townhouse for a year or so— thanks largely to our misunderstanding the realtor & thinking the tapas bar across the street was *topless*— I can tell you these pictures are typically executed in about the time it takes him to smoke a Marlboro Red or for Nick Cave to tear through his cover of "Black Betty" (bam-ba-*lam*), Thaddeus signing each of them like an explorer planting Old Glory into some new lunar golf course. As for academic prizes & accolades, let's just say the only blue ribbon to interest this self-taught re-naissance man is made by Pabst. As for a price tag, well, T-boy would rather give you a drawing gratis, for, were he to charge what it cost him, you couldn't begin to afford it, Cap'n.

—David Rowe
New Orleans, 2008

for those who will have it
but have not had it

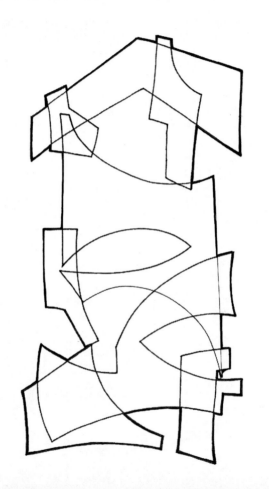

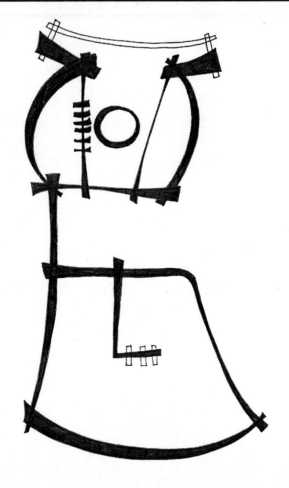

PLEASE DON'T TAKE AWAY MY PENS

        it   is
only

                        so safe   to dream

  only so safe
  only   so safe

it is only so safe to dream

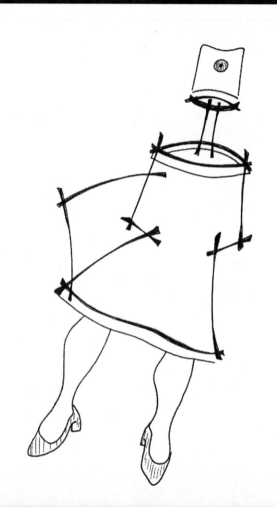

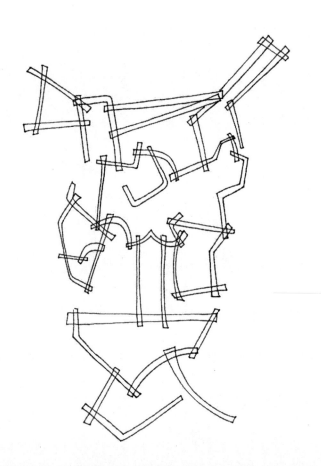

respect my genuflect   eat your spam and

resurrect

 is the unknown anything   similar to not

knowing
            what theorem to   postulate
or
            which pig to castrate

for the   feast

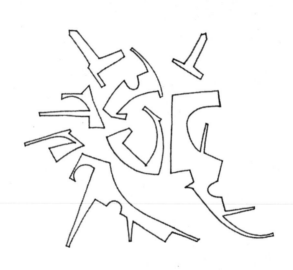

WORDING THIS WAD

Hmmmmshastic
    the   tune to   hum   is frantic

resting   on velvet
in the darkness   of a dresser

            sits a diamond empty

of everything but itself

meditate on some other truth

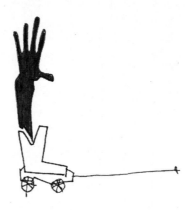

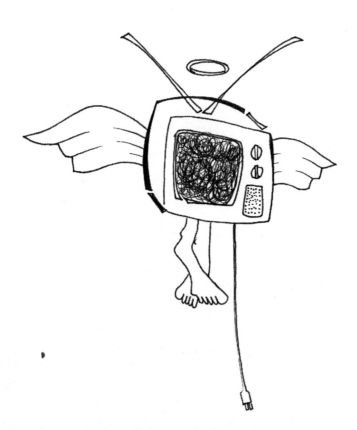

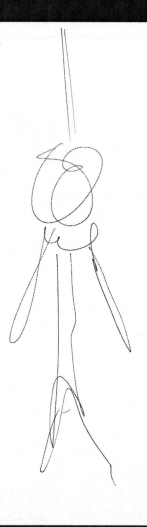

KANT O' KNEES

communism is real I guess
about as real   as   liver cheese sandwiches

which reminds me of a story

            that   almost sounds

    nostalgic

                let's give it a minute

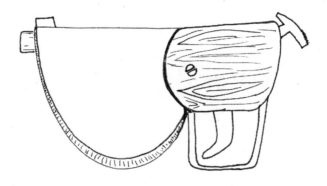

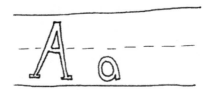

RAMSHOOKEN

when will I find   the
                time
for the books   I   have   misread
the   schools I've misrepresented

when will my cume be full

and what   is the next era of   video game

DESDELLAMA

if I'm   to be up in the
   morning
then I stay

                          out all night
in a deduction   of misinstruction
   mustard minus peas

          corn can holds the universe in check

when the time comes
               to distill   all our prayer
for a nonlinear life

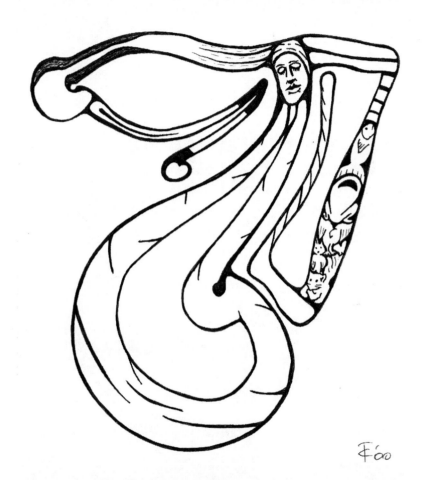

GIVING THE GAVE TO GET WHAT YOU GOT

have it this   way

  crumble

        jumble
            pick up sticks

                                    the salad
bar is

full of geriatrics
who as children found Saturday after their favorite cartoons

                        somewhat useless

GENERIC POETRY

transylvania is proliferated
  by a series
      of

                                    cumstains

left undetected
by

the planned parenthood   and other
ex-strangle-holes

                              i.e. ted nugent

GENUFAKE

there they were
snails   in   the   last row

            of a church
where   infinity had begun again
as a watch word

with too   many

                              consonants for
anything but scrabble

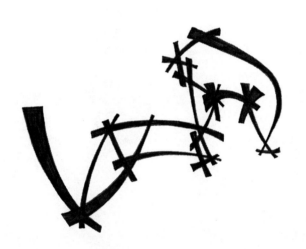

THE MANY WAYS TO READ A WORD

after   untying so many

                knots
my mind works   just fine
                        pinball visions
        that   mar the tender   page
                are reluctant attempts
at lemonade

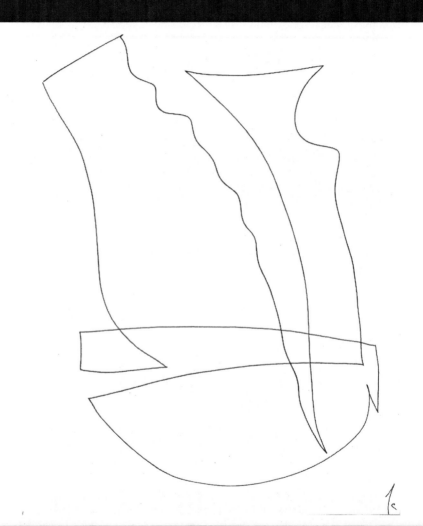

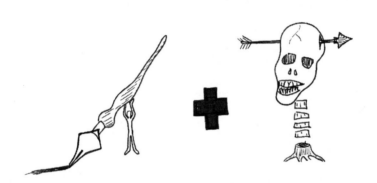

1c

ON PRAYERS BEING ANSWERED

if life is suffering
we're   in luck
because
  luck don't time
  time don't look
and god knows all of santa's   miscalculations

POP U LURCH

the blues
will   eat you up
till
you   got nothing
 just as well as when you get
                                              done

with   having   nothing

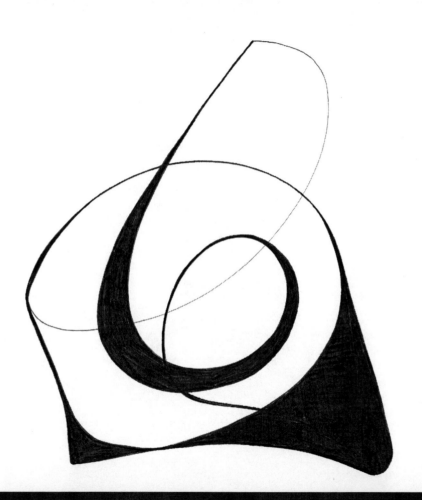

CONSUME THE MOON

if the ifs
turn brown   in some
incest of the high type
cast on armadillo
                I will revenge with aste spumante

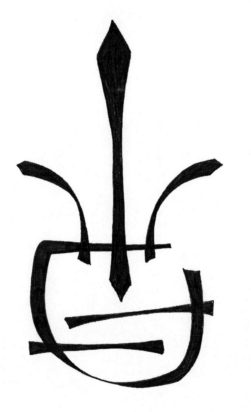

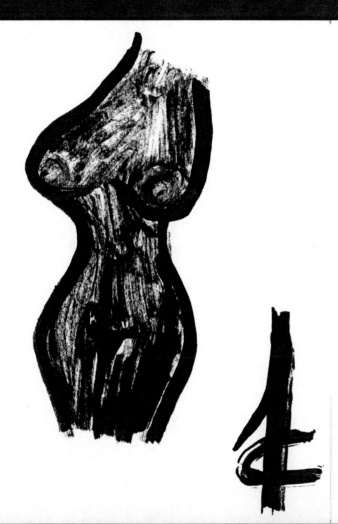

BAD NEWS SUNSHINE

courting   is not   what it   once   was
times of
antiquazi fornitado

english   must die

to wholly be the priestly language
ginsberg   was awarded a silk rose for his efforts

          there is a frame at the convenience store for

employee   of the month
which   is empty

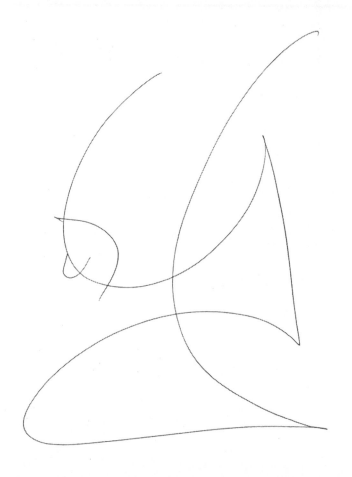

UNTRUE MELODY

allsome in the raven night   cool   greens sleep in varied greys
until the sun reveals   a war of shadows rise
with hope to depart

only
to fall
back   into the horizon
at dusk

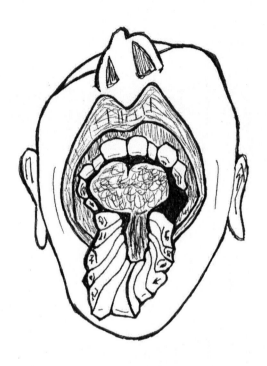

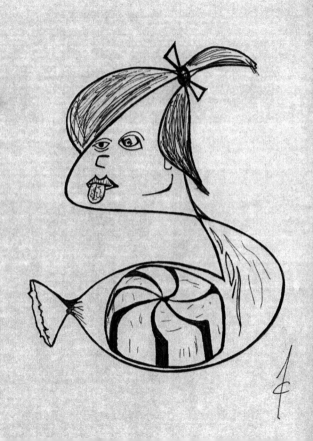

SHUT UP AND WRITE A BOOK

one needs to want
too want
duality is symbiosis

intellectuals feed   on unshed tears

whereas a dog has the sense   to sweat from
          his mouth

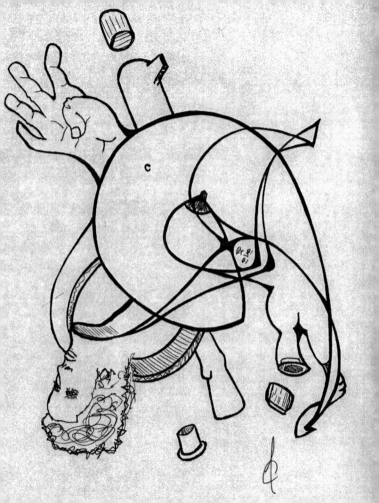

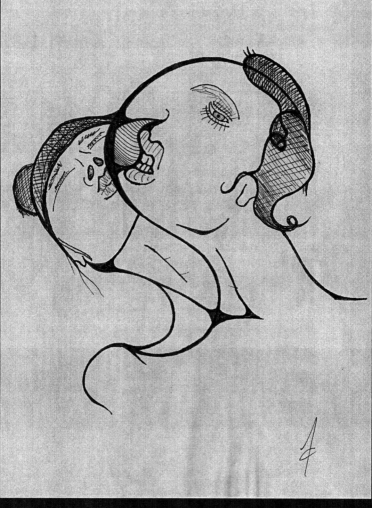

WARRANT APPLIED FOR

    short of some shower stall punk game

there are
     bars on most   flags
friday
we aim   our   rifles at the moon
and Monday we pin our focus to the heels in front of us

it's no surprise
that I have no point

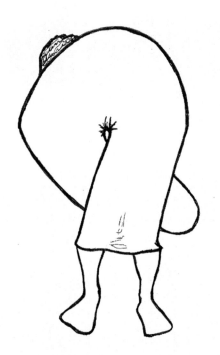

PASS THE BOTTLE ARISTOPHANES

        cunt   re: music
fox   paws
                        like dirty draws

the past will never happen

4'03

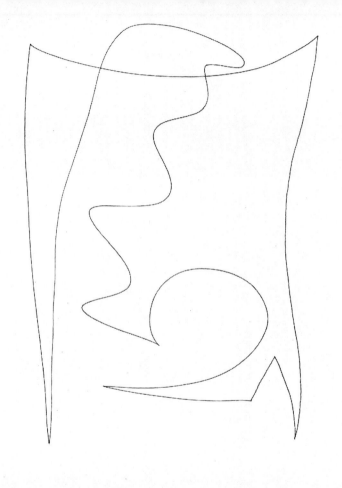

1c

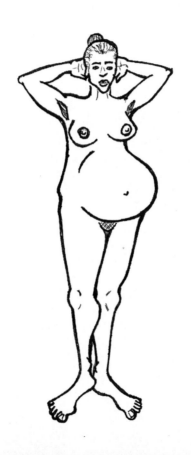

SUBTITULARITY

we are mere
                reflecting pools   of moon dip honey sunshine
that gum   the teeth of a savage deity named time

1c

1c

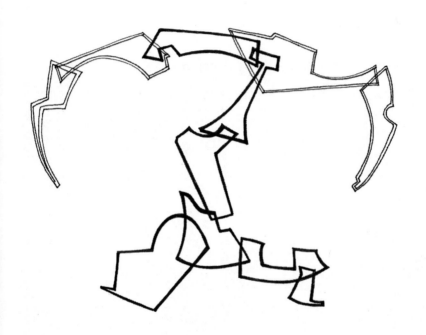

art is a   residual
of   unseen disaster
a wound sufficiently   drained of pus
power   or both

an infidel may grease the mechanism proper
                    such as a
                                    mattress dumb

opera   dreaming

poet

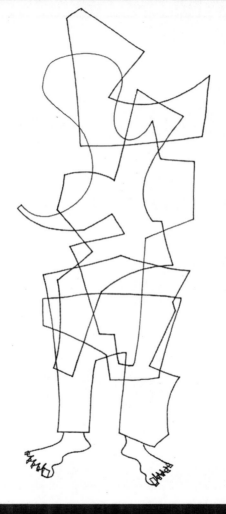

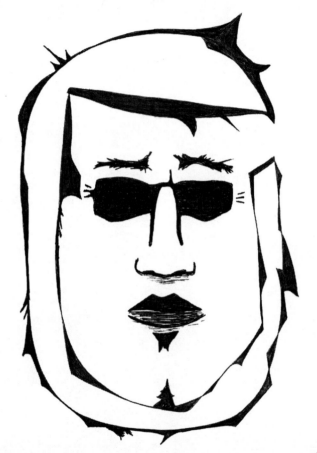

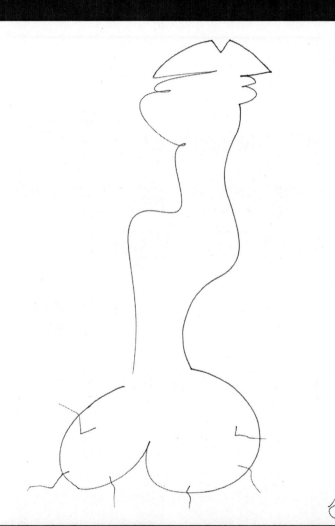

I

music   is   music
from aerosol junkies   to   art school
flunkies
kubla camp   kiche kind
neither is there more matter than space
nor space than time

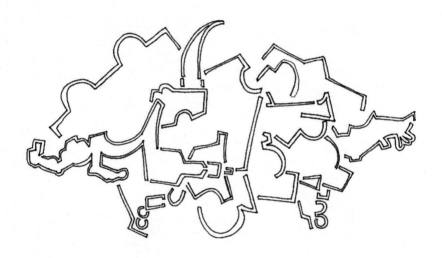

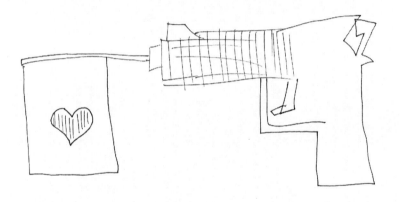

4

STERILE

      my   country   tis of
fear
    sweet and nasty   cheap   but pratical

prometheus   cannot comprehend the differences
      between   free
or   stolen

when there   is no fork in the pan

or a cure   for his cancer

PROFILES OF ZERO

there   square in a   shit-storm
sat   Herodotus
                                    clamoring

to his shriveled cock

with a greased palm

                                    after having greased
the cornice   tits of Venus

 although his trajectory was miscalculated
        as were the   hip replacements
meant for mentoring
in a glue fumed vision on ice skates
the rosy cheeked wise-cracker
smeared
his dentures with lipstick before uttering the words

                                    he knew so well

PATRIOTIC EMBOLISM

although every   note should be   cherished
    tomorrow   stares into a dreamish halfism
 as we all misappropriate
heartfelt   yet mis pronounced diagnosi

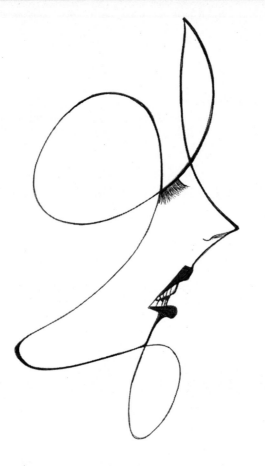

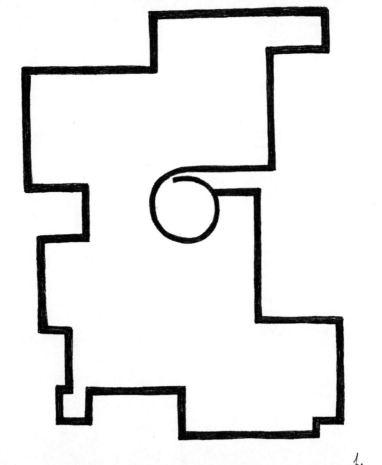

WE ARE THE ALIENS

when music meets music and   the true music
          is chosen
to displace
that which music displaces

I then say to myself   as if I was someone
          else

                    you are the trespasser

REDUX

this city sleeps in the ugly fun   of   comfort and
                misery
I will bring you here
 we will   live out our poor judgment because what is past
is unimportant

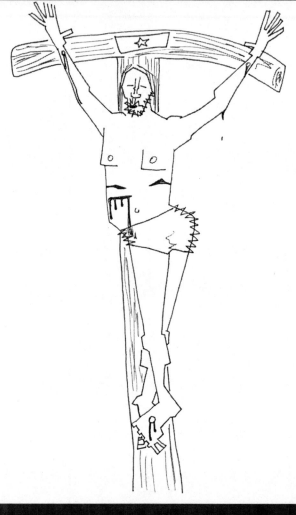

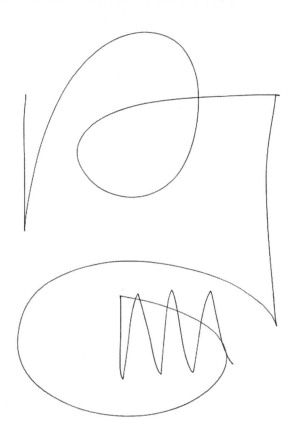

ADDENDUM TO GET AN ATHEIST INTO HEAVEN

we   are   imperfect nonthings

once   when we did not exist

we   were   perfect

immaculate

now   that we have   come
from the place   where secrets   are   kept
we are   promethean

sanctioned conscious   illuminated dirt
students of the mass hallucination that is time
 in god
and   the   god
that does not exist
is perfect

to regard god as a nonentity
is to revere   his absolute perfection

THE DIFFERENCE BETWEEN FOREIGN FILMS AND DOMESTIC DRUG USE

as a modern   practitioner   of   magic
and a fan
of fellini
making fish jump out of the toilet
after   flushing

a tampon along   with aspirin and antacid

that have past their expiration

                                    does not surprise me
                  in the   least

but as a trustee   of recreational chemistry

I refuse to kill the bugs that crawl out of my arm

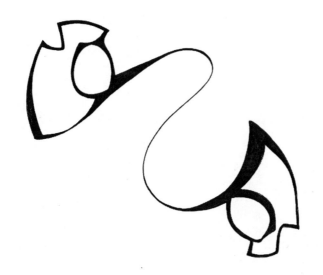

⌐4'03

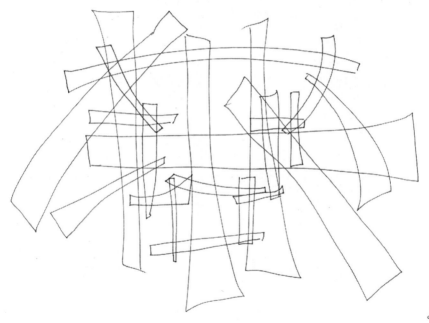

FRAGGING COLONEL MUSTER

sins and dreams
dereliction

soccer moms don't just not take it in the ass
                        doing their diamond duty

            they expect you not to think of it
when they are hunched over
grunting

strapping their child into the car seat

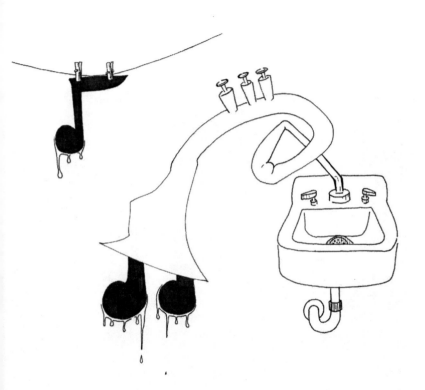

1

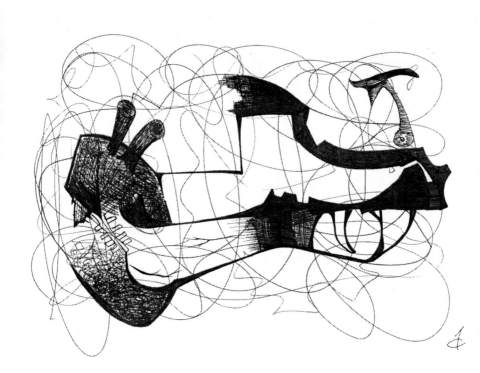

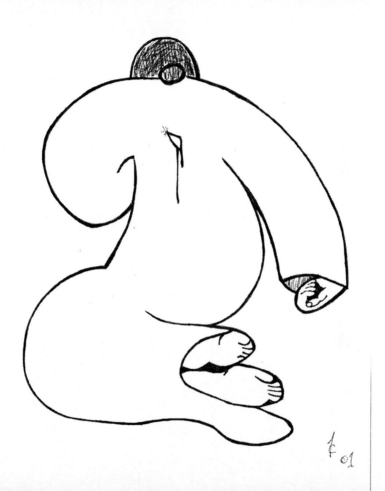

A PREEMPTIVE MEETING OF ALCHOHOLICS ANONYMOUS AT THE
SATELLITE GRAVESITE OF LORD BYRON WITHOUT THE PERMISSION OF HIS
ESTATE OR THE KNOWLEDGE OF THE GENERAL SERVICE COMMITTEE

confessing the blues
loose shoes
this tight prayer of a pussy   vomits   forth
                                                          the world

all worry relies on fear

and my fear rests   upon the precipice   of an

enema clip
but frankly speaking let us hope that the strings on my violin hold fast

after all the best songs are
the sad

ones

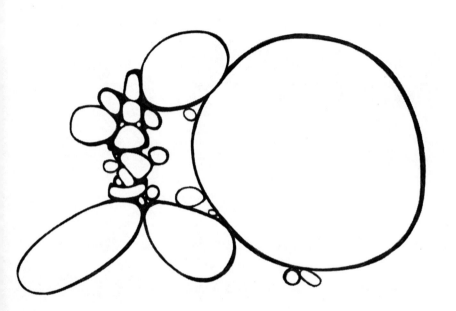

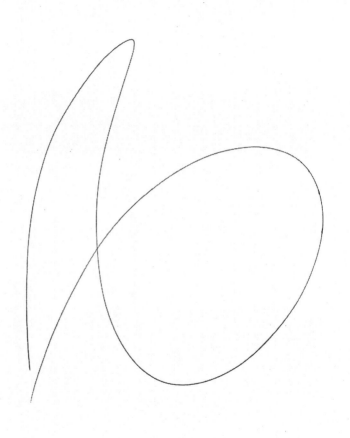

ALL I EVER NEEDED TO KNOW I LEARNED IN THOSE FIRST FEW HOURS AT
REHAB

voted most likely to succeed in high school
and thinking this would buy credence

with the drug counselors
                        I poured my heart into the first couple of hours
         there
but when the drugs wore off
                         I signed myself out

IMPETUS

when the acid kicks in
and your teeth turn into grape jell-o
do not bite your lip
you silly fuck

TREASON IN VAUDEVILLE

I find it hard to say what I mean
but   it is a flaw   that I have use for

                              seeing that I lie incessantly

about the size   of my penis

and   my years   in the service

I am   waiting to be blindfolded

                                    backed against
a wall
handed a cigarette

              where and when I will lift my hand

before bowing
to tell the onlookers it was all a joke

THE HEART IS NOT A PIMPLE

I am   swearing off emotions

settling   for the   limited joy   of
denying   my feelings

as for this moment

you will not find me   wasting it   writing   this   poem

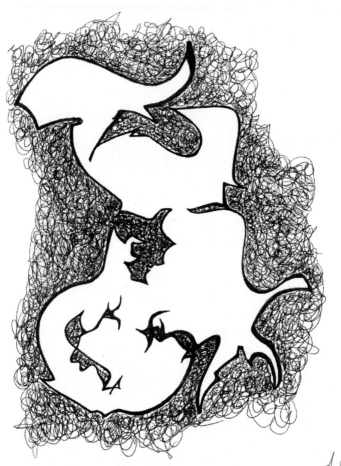

PLASTIC IS THE COTTON OF THE TWENTY FIRST CENTURY

before there was   nothing
                everything was something

    but   now that

                                nothing is something

everything   is the same

and   even I get tired of drugs
and classical   music

that does not mean the miracle
                    isn't right around the corner

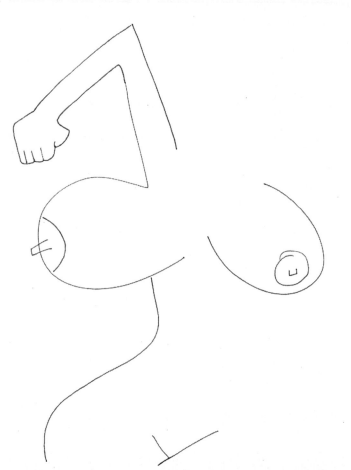

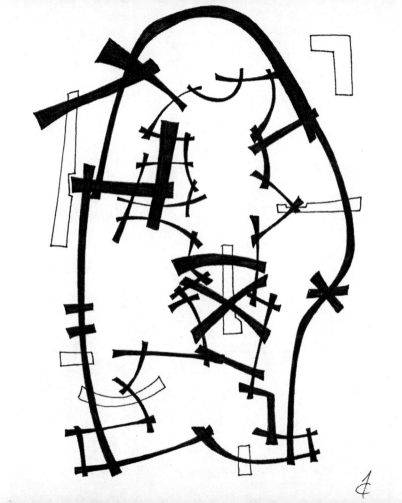

SHAMANABALISTIC

tell the world   that   you
ride out poison
             in the clutter of   a dirty room

the wrong poison

dreaming of the day   that you are choking

on the small breast   of some ballerina

neither drink the antidote

nor stay   in compliance   with certain federal statutes

after all you command the dusty yellowed pages
of light and love

tell the world that you are a poet
and when you see the question in its eyes

answer yes

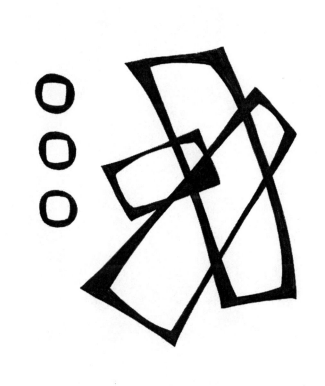

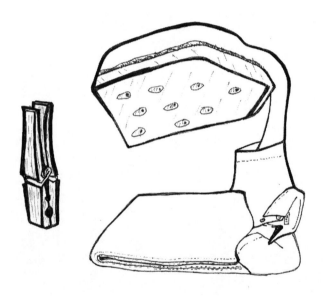

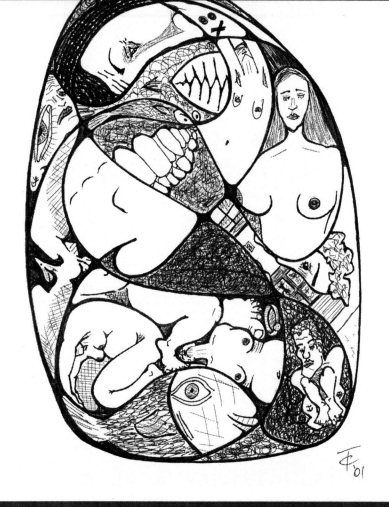

THE DEMYSTIFICATION OF AN AMERICAN TEENAGER TURNED MAN

lately I don't feel like   masturbating
on my   coffee break

I just think about old girlfriends and high school

once   I took a five   off a table
at pizza   hut

it was not   for me   but   I took it anyway

I suspect something of steadily fucking a   hole in my chi

if it is   the worm of conscience

                              then

                                        why

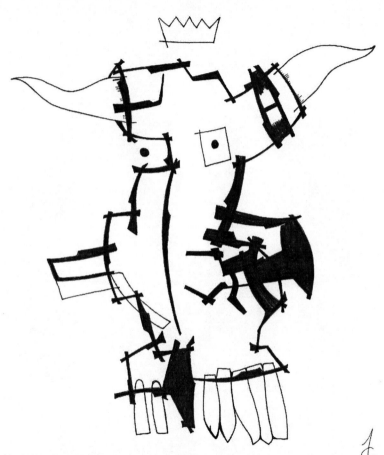

A EUCLIDIAN RECIPE OF ARTIFICIAL SUNLIGHT FOR THE SPLINTERED
CONTINGENCY OF PENTHOUSE FORUM SUBSCRIBERS

when the   trap   door   opens
and   the   cartoon   character
                  has yet to realize   it

what is it   that holds him up

faith   grace   will
                        this argument remains unanswered
            from   scholars   to stoners

generally   the injured reasoning   of ignorance
and   lust

will often   leave   more than just some
dirty sheets
and I have never   understood   or

been   persuaded   by satin

for romance   is no bruised vegetable

romantics   die

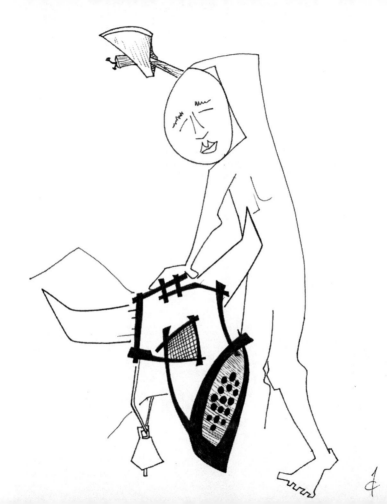

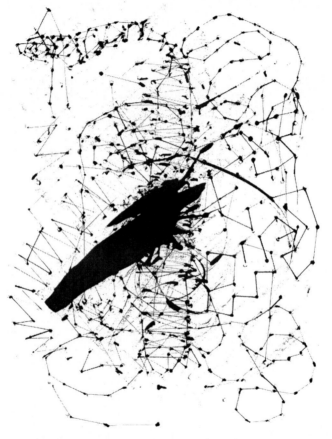

THE SEXUAL PROWESS OF A METEOROLOGIST AS HELD OVER FROM THE
AGE OF AQUARIUS

one should practice gentle   addictions
have a sense of the
maladjusted

so when those   around them   step out of the norm
they can reign them in   as well as help them cultivate
a sense   of shame
                         it is all too easy
                         to wield a scalpel

in this world of sores

if I were a musician   I would suspend
          theory

and call upon
the absence of certain   knowledges   to write

                              our song

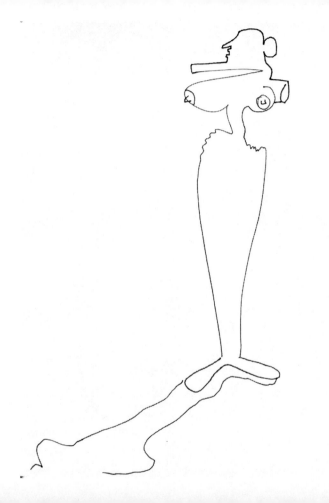

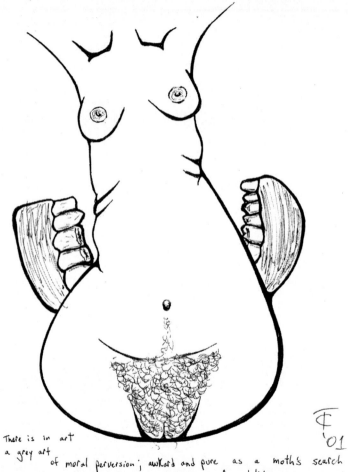

There is in art
a grey art
of moral perversion; awkward and pure as a moth's search
for deliverance.

IN TIMES AS THESE

behavior addicts
should all own dogs
be put to task on setting up
                              dog show obstacle courses
as well as the rules and regulations for such events
this
and they
should beat their children openly at the grocery
where everyone can see their true colors

although this would create wild gangs of runaways

it would help the long suffering white slave trade
and   create one hell of a dog show

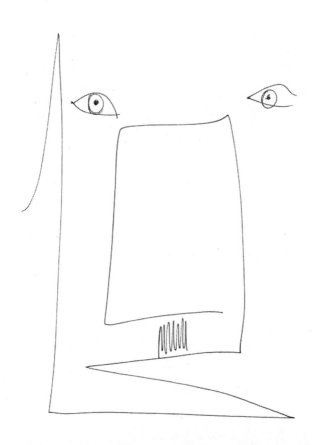

APPRENTICESHIP AS A REASON TO RIDE

let me tell you about them
they have nothing to contribute
they are worthless
they refused to get into the
big white van
climb into the big white van
I'll take the roll of carpet out
then you can bring a friend

I'll take the highway
and we'll get there quicker
we'll be in a rush to see everything
it's all about observations
we'll untie the minutes from the darkness
there are no windows in the big white van
a white van with windows is as useless as its passengers
derelicts on their way to detox
those with down's syndrome on a day pass
and of course Baptists
climb into the big white van
I know what you think
I know what you've heard
but everything I've ever learned
I learned in the big white van
there is rope in the big white van

rope comes in handy
climb into the big white van
all your dreams are true
and I dream too
we'll go around like a broken shopping cart
no one will suspect our talents
everyone will underestimate us
after all we're in the big white van
we'll be doing research
we'll be observers
doing constant research
you don't do research on the top floor
of some swank fucking building
you do it on the street
down alleys
in a big white van
climb into the big white van
we'll set the controls for the heart of the ghetto
we'll drive by vacant lots with tall grass and abandoned mattresses
fuck we might even stop
climb into the big white van
we'll arm ourselves with several phrases
such as
it's not my fault
you're the one that's crazy
and the staple of being in the big white van
which is

*

climb into the big white van
we'll have a chance at ruining their world

don't be like they are
don't be like them

they are afraid to give half a fucking try
me
I'm fully aware of trying
and I have nothing to hide
after all I climbed into the big white van
it is a sin to be unwilling to fuck it up for everyone
when there is a chance we might get it right
there is no blame in the big white van
it is not us
it is not our perception of them
it is them
they refused to climb into the big white van
there are worse fates than climbing into the big white van
so climb into the big white van
and we'll kick down the door to eternity

CRACK

there is a
chance I won't need nothing
there is a chance I won't need next there is a
chance above all reasons
reasons why and why and why and why

I went where the floor squeaks
into the room where my grandmother sleeps
and the floor creaks   it is my grandmother's room
this house is old
it is an old house
and the floor squeaks
you think differently when it's   dark
and you're being sneaky
you oversimplify the obvious
and
the last thing you want to hear is her stop breathing
it means she's about to wake up

I
grab the bible
and open to the pages where money once was

it has remembered the
place it once

WAS

and all the costume jewelry in her second to last drawer
will neither bring it back

nor unmuffle the profanities I whisper

while wishing I were dead

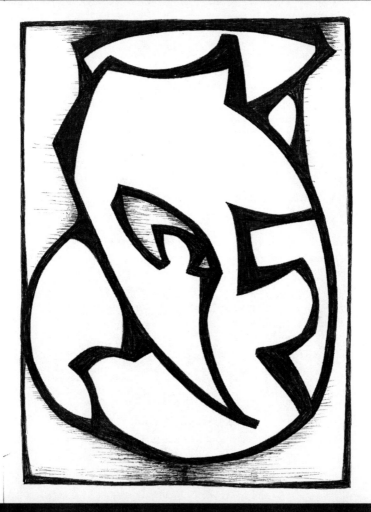

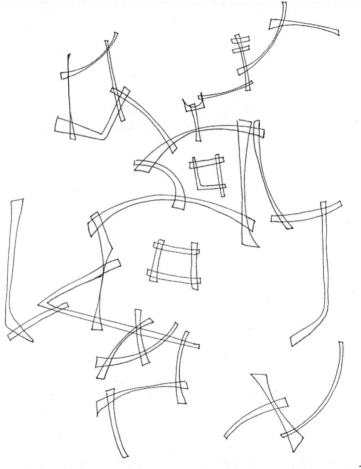

HIGHLY UNSCIENTIFIC SEARCH FOR SIGNS OF THE OVERSOUL

maybe I am a hard case
after all I do like to look in the toilet when I'm finished
however the psychology behind not flushing eludes me
I enjoy flushing
it is as though I am destroying that which I have created

I let my cigarettes live out their ash
in the crux between the curb and the street
until the cherry whimpers

I might even languor and muse about the possible destruction of a
          city
by way of my callous disposal of things

only because I have found myself on an odd corner
now and then
alone
to skip and scrape my cheap shoes on the concrete
where the reciprocal of my collected sighs
are spent
in a single laugh

TREATISE

I used to know when I was finished with writing something
because I wanted to kill myself
this made editing my writing
pretty fucking easy
I guess it was a compliment to myself
as if cashing in all the chips simply
to let the work speak for itself
was a just exit

when I first resigned myself to being a writer
I would sit at my desk and the only
word that I could think of was "death"

I would avoid writing this
then write words such as
"love" "soul" and "joy"

but I rarely knew what I meant

some days I think of giving up writing
I wake after having slept all night
feeling tired and useless
as though no rest was had

the thing I neglect to remember in those minutes
is that when I want to live die love or scream
I usually grab for a pen

KNOWING THE SUBTLE CONGRUENCY BETWEEN NEED AND WANT

some dreams are true

hungry toilets and faggots know
that
public restrooms have insatiable appetites for the crudest of

drama
Liberace was not a hemorrhoidic effigy to the
counter culture

and not all pirates have one eye

nor does all sin involve joy

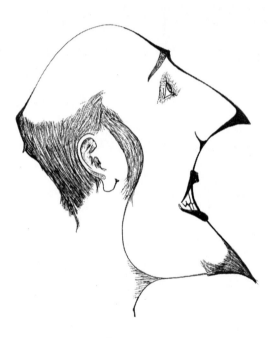

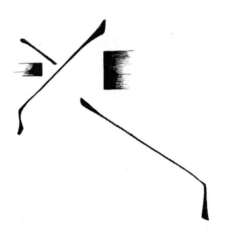

LIGHTING A MATCH BEHIND BINOCULARS IN AN ELEVATOR SHAFT

projecting attitudes onto the unevolved
may be a problem for some

my karma isn't square

and I dislike everyone in one way or another

maybe I should run for public office

seeing as I
dislike myself

then when the issues are presented

I could work song lyrics into the conversation

seeming   witty

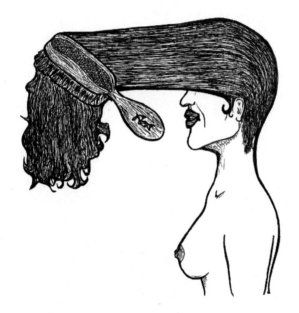

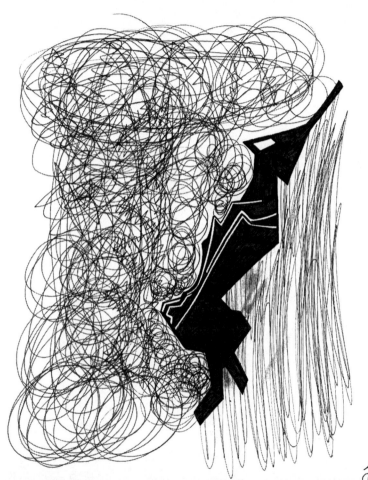

TALENT IS NOT A PRECURSOR TO SANITY

the spirits of the air

aren't known to cut corners   on the
            production
value

of my dreams

never is there a microphone   in view

                        and their edits are seamless

                they are evidently   highly ethical
        technicians

        but

        sometimes

                                        their choice of
        subject matter

                wakes me up

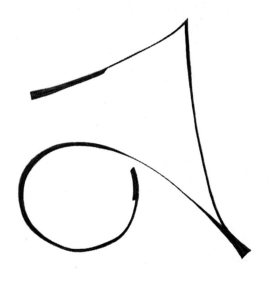

ASTROGLIDE FOR ASTRAL PLANE

grease the dream

with margarine

                                                            postage sufficient:
            oblivion
                        past the moon   it's not his business

the infinite inventory of wishes

                                                if

it
            lay

            unanswered

in   this   ever
            expanding
universe

rotting vile   past   original intent

tie it to a brick

and   challenge hope in a shallow
            puddle

THE GENERAL IMPLICATION OF BEING

try to find the place where all systems converge in the
            light
open

a   bank   account   with
them

try not to look nervous
and if they ask for references
                              run for the woods with a stack of withdrawal
            slips

                        just because all your girlfriends fathers never
            trusted you

                                                doesn't mean you're a
            bad guy

                                        but they usually know about
            these things

nevertheless
            it will make for a good back-story when the dogs are called off
                                                and some girl chooses to
            help you

THE BISHOP OF CANTILEVER AND THE MALARIA SYMPHONIES

just so long as you mean it
it doesn't matter what you do

                              as long as it has feeling
          feeling fucking   trumps a
            plumb heart

tell me that   you never loved me

                                            burn holes

        in my shit

call my friends and tell them
I can't get it up

fuck anonymous men who pretend to console you

it doesn't matter what you do

                                        just so long as

        you mean it

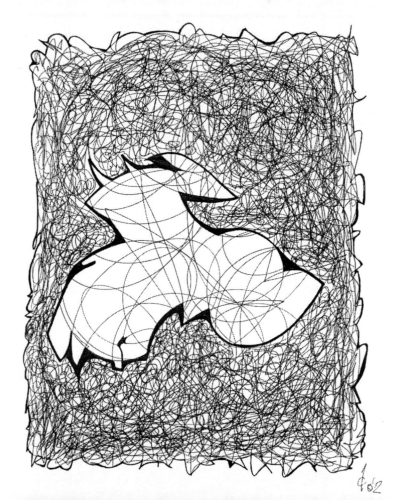

SEEMINGLY IMPOSSIBLE RETALIATION ON THE INCREDIBLE HULK BY
BEETHOVEN AND THE SONATAS THAT FOLLOWED

structured benevolence is all
that unconditional love   is   for kittens

even when salmon enters   the
        picture

sodomy has lost its city
they bartered it for infamy

sex   is not a tributary

       of love

how   can   I   have   any   thing
      else   to
say

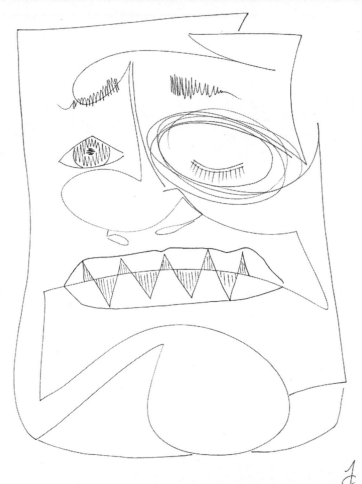

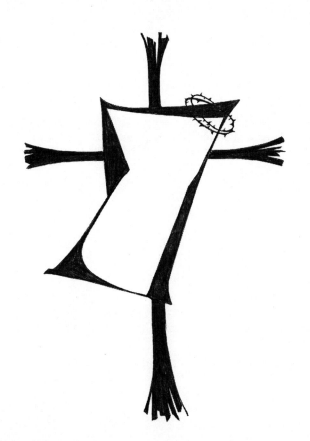

OUT WITH AN ELEPHANT EYE

although no one man should have to bare this burden
and with stern prejudice

neither do I take pleasure in nor am I consoled
by the following

but in strict abeyance for my chosen profession
it is my duty as well as my deepest shame to inform the public

that as of noon tomorrow

Thaddeus Conti
will have sold out

it is true I Thaddeus Conti
being above reproach and beyond the scope of the average mind
have chosen to cash in

first thing will be to make all of those who once supported me
feel alienated
then I will phone it in from there
the actual procedure of how I chose to ruin my good name
as an artist
is
of little consequence

it should be noted
that my integrity tact and values
will not have changed I will simply let you see who I really am

yours truly

T

DISCLOSING VISIONS TO SEMI-PERMANENT STRANGERS

altars built in the absence of faith   love   or money

have little purpose in worshipping anything
        but musicians   that   have had
an untimely end

pistol grip shotgun talk of making it famous or else

only pays off

        when a teenage girl needs

        a reason to

        light
        candles

THE INVERSE RATIO OF FELLATIO TO MIGRANT PROSTITUTES

sucking dick
as if to eliminate unemployment   alleviate the jones

                                                        nomad
          whores

have more heart
               than
hips   more trouble

than treble

                         pawn the dream
               cause when   our

                                                        ship
          comes

down the   yellow
          bricks

of   ghettoville

we'll pay the interest   in shake

INVITE TO THE PESTILENT

America soda pops a bubble in every eye around the globe
it propagates no lies   America is what it is and it lives

        as a child who played his video games dutifully
by Christ
                                I am a qualified American

I hereby invite all to come to America
the big bad wolf salivating hungry

where the eye looks it sees and you'll see America

                        what does it mean to remember
it will be a fucking sad affair when they close the door
    who's going to marry the unwanted
    who's going to fix all these broke down cars
    who's going to understand
all the angels with emotional issues are down a dark
road on
the side of the airport

where the truth is
where America lives

fine dining dilettantes
class distinct
debauchees
dirt hearted debutantes

don't touch my America
fuck those hyper driving web linking shit fuckers
I will not waste a polaroid on their America

I'll give you my America
a let me fuck you like it's the fourth of July America
with a tomato in your cunt and a sparkler in your hand
screaming
 give me a reason to want to be free

legalize sodomy

we'll find a farm hand willing to cook up a bunch of speed
and we'll   feel shame in the sunlight   picking scabs
          where we
cut our wrists   feigning injuries to avoid
          imprisonment
                    sitting next to a Native American putting
          cigarettes out on her arm

we'll take back the innocent America   the naive fucks on

      the first date America
and turn it into an identity thieving cleavage bearing knife fight with
      someone who's willing to cheat on his taxes America all the
      middle age adolescents will be scoring and waiting for the
      odd waitress who likes to dance to get off work from a shitty
      job so they
can get the
odd blow job America

and we'll be close to something
like a red eyed trucker the lot lizard's lunch depends on
and lunch is just another hit America
               what of ideals
someone says who deals   down on the carpet burning
      knees I'll take a light beer and a handful of these
a dollar's worth   a
      dollar's worth

make it a hundred dollars' worth

               God damn it this is America

               buffets free delivery
          everybody's' dream ends in 99 cents

I promise adultery

adulterated adults acting like kids to get what they want
and when it's Christmas
they'll step on wrists and throats to get the biggest
fucking toy for their brat
that's America
I'll be damned if it's dead
America lives
in a full on black out making a turn well past the required
speed limit
so don't worry about the radio station
America lives

                                        in the scratched out
              serial numbers on a 9 millimeter
in a cop killing
plotting looting pirating conspiring
homeless homesick America
founded by revolution
unresolved from the greatness of the villains who went before us
so pack your bags and prepare to vilify the sacred
                        because

              empathy is obsolete

              and America lives

LIBRANOIA

on the outside of town
in the basement of the big factory
there is a man with a key and a gun
who sits behind a button in his denim coveralls

the man who sits before the button is no dreamer
he does not daydream
he is a tool
he has a job to do

he is not distracted by the millions of flashing green lights

he does not wonder what he will have for lunch
or if he will be fucked this very evening
his attention is solely on the button

when the button flashes red he must push it

he is fully prepared to shut the whole fucking operation down

on first glance the factory appears to produce raspberry spray air
            freshener

its true function is
the bastardization of philosophical ideas

and the pasteurization of current events

I am not at liberty or willing to divulge more than this
 the key is for the door
 the gun is for intruders
and the button simply shuts down the whole fucking operation

as I said this man does not daydream
 he is in control after all he is ultimately responsible for our thoughts

if something that is too dangerous to be processed is presented
 the button will blink red

the man in denim coveralls will push that button
he will secure the door
 chamber a round
 and wait

if the machine shuts down
for more than five seconds
a light will blink in washington dc
a phone will ring
and someone is to be awoken from a sound sleep

the man in dc dreams of the phone call
and red buttons make his asshole wink
he has been trained

he knows exactly what to do
 he does not have to be briefed
he does not have to be told
 what the idea was
or what the current event happened to be

he simply knows that the factory must be on line

the man in dc orders the machine to be purged the idea to be
            eradicated the event to have never have happened

although he might have to shit
after all the excitement
he usually goes back to bed unfettered

books then go missing at libraries

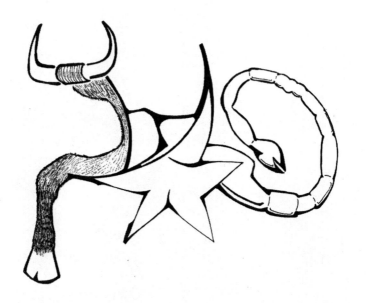

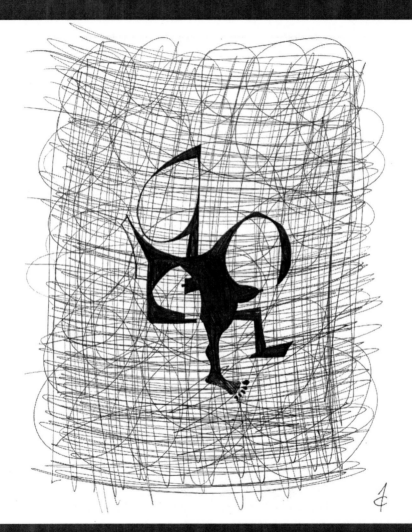

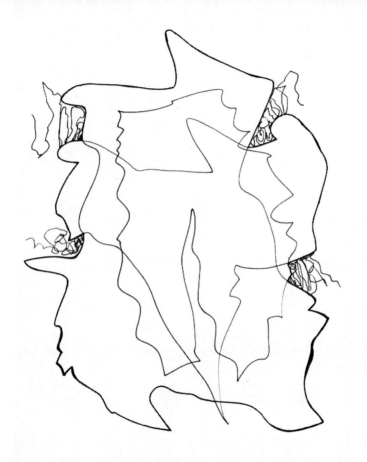

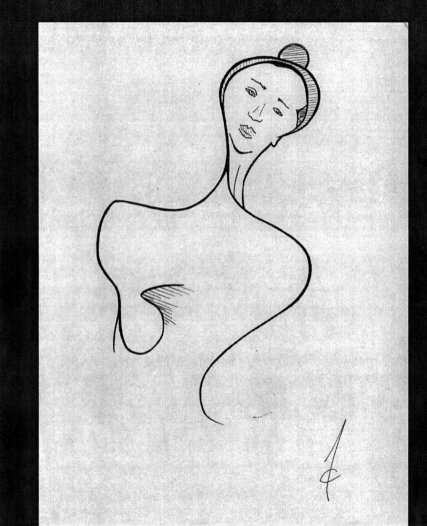

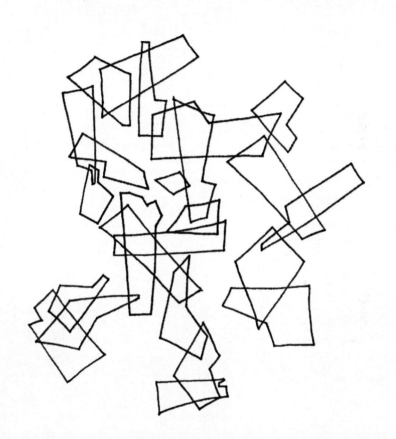